MUD FOREWORD

If a picture is worth a thousand words, my stories are like a million words long. I'm an artist with experience in illustration, graphic design, comics, animation and everything in between.

I've been working on indie comic books and doing freelance work for the better part of a decade, improving my skills and trying to get my name out there. I'm very passionate about telling stories through art and when ever I start a project I like to see it through to the end.

I've worked with the comic book publishers as well as started my own studio. In this book I'm going to show you some great art and I'm going to teach you what I know.

CHRIS GOODING
ARTIST

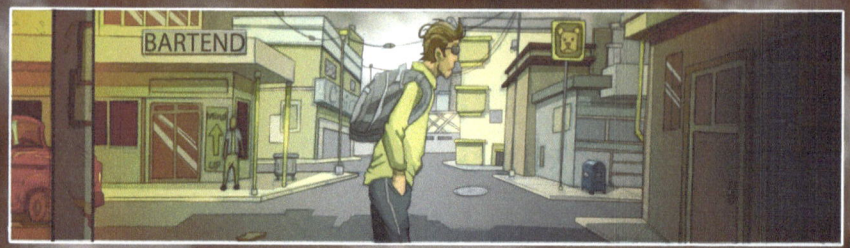
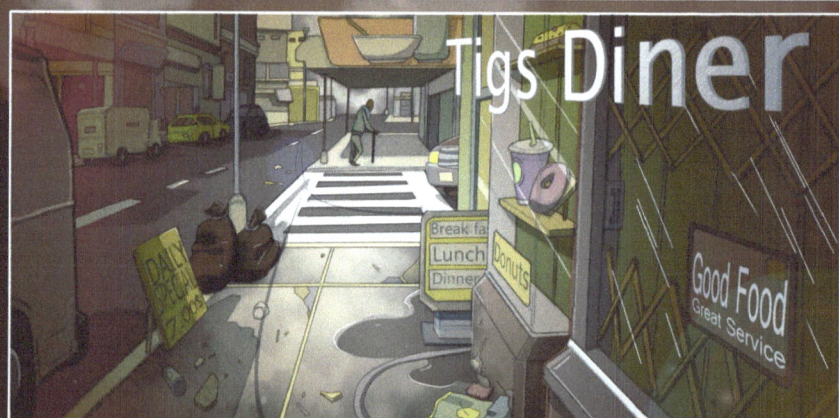
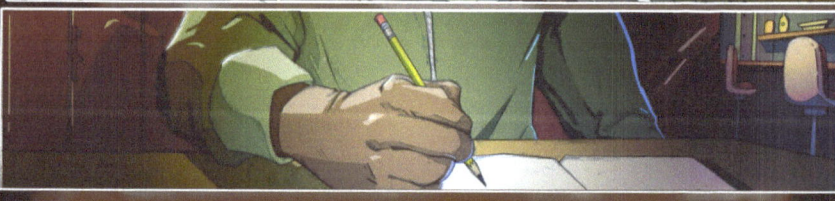
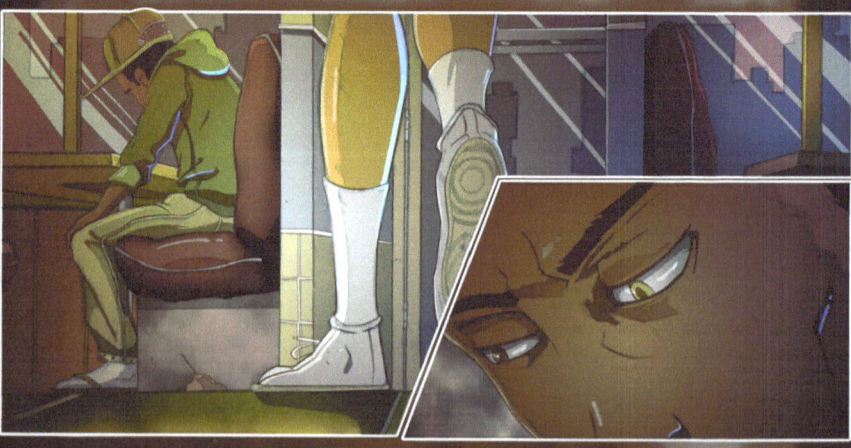

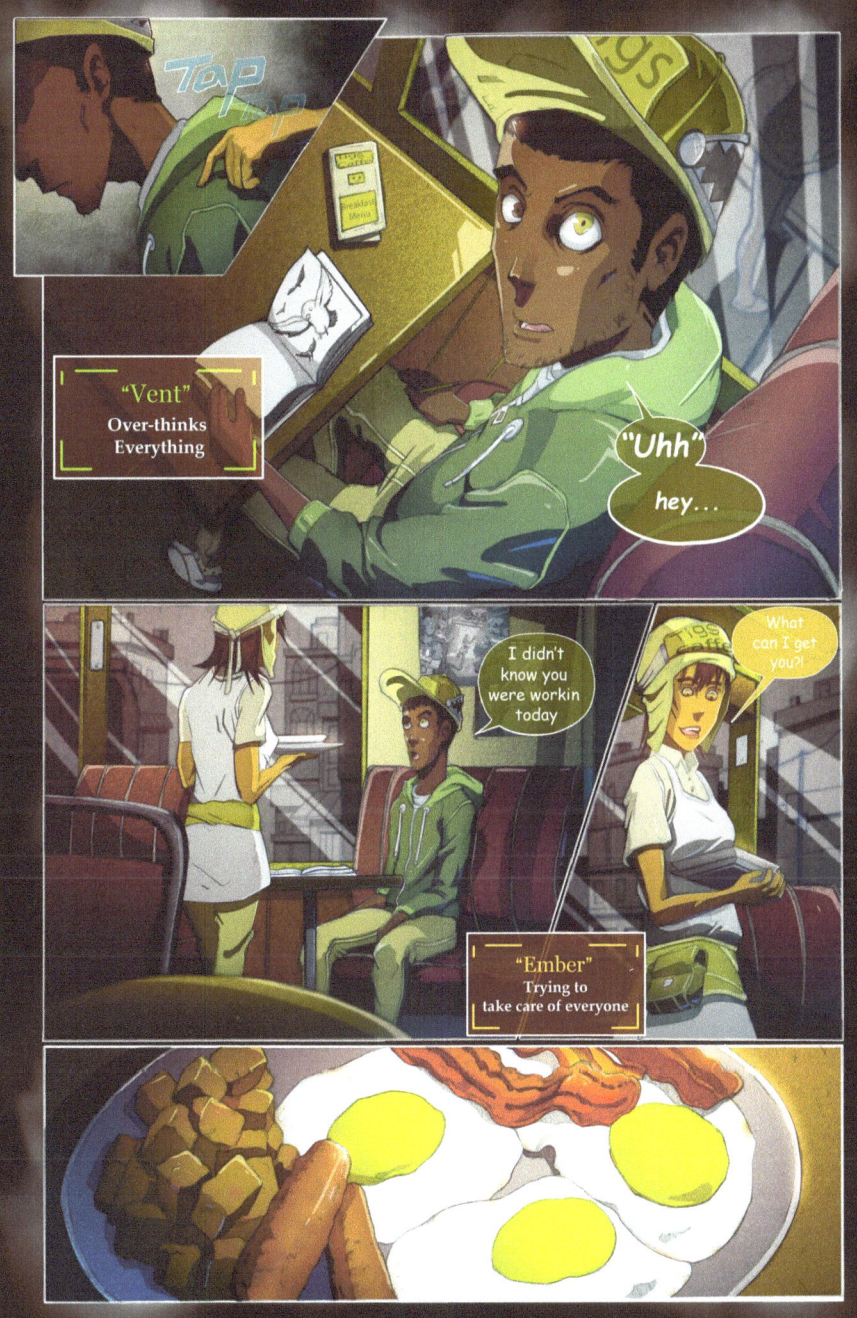

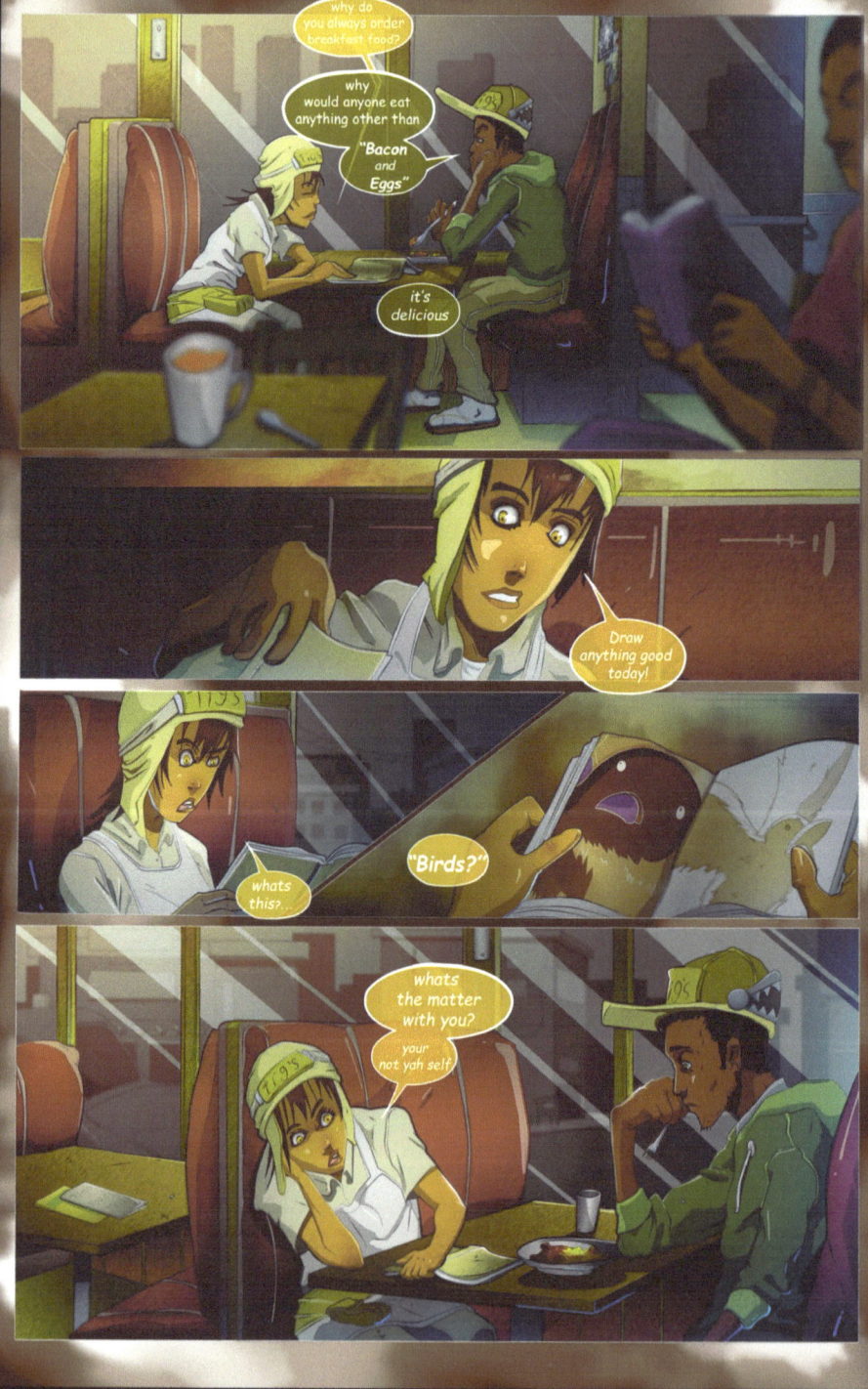

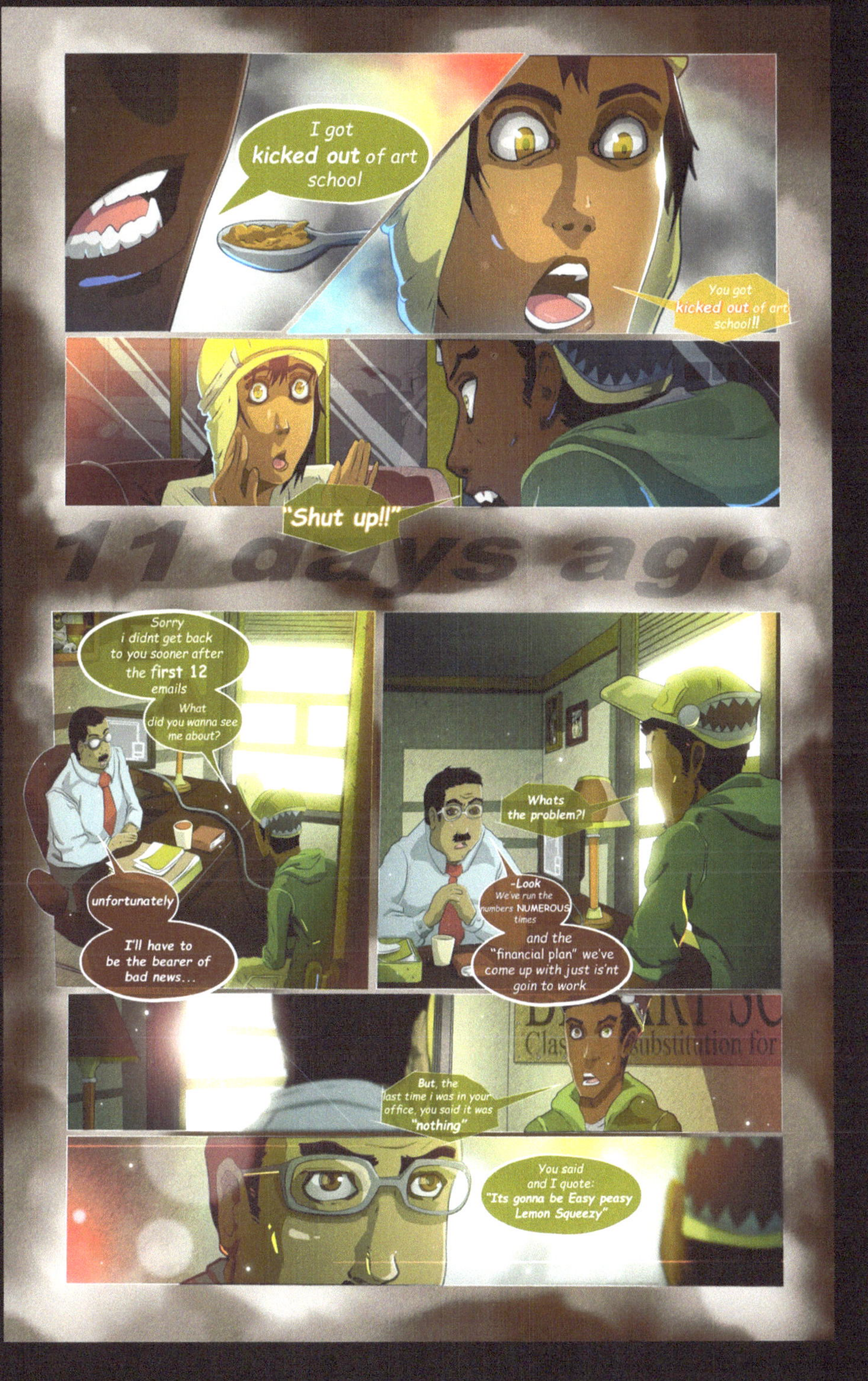

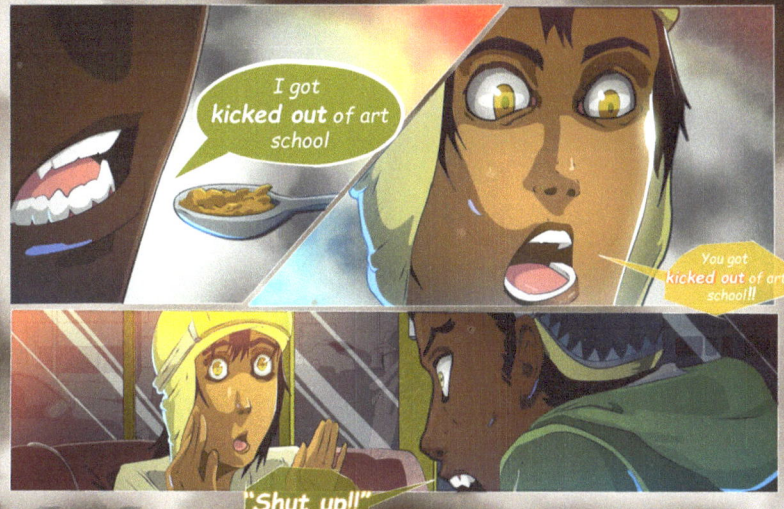

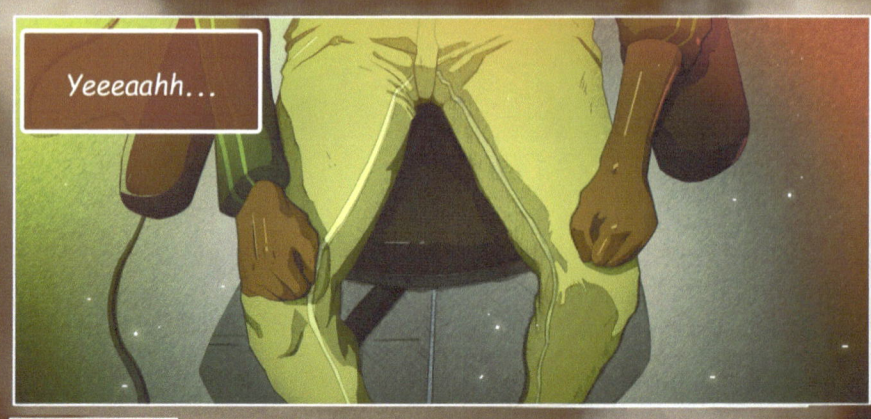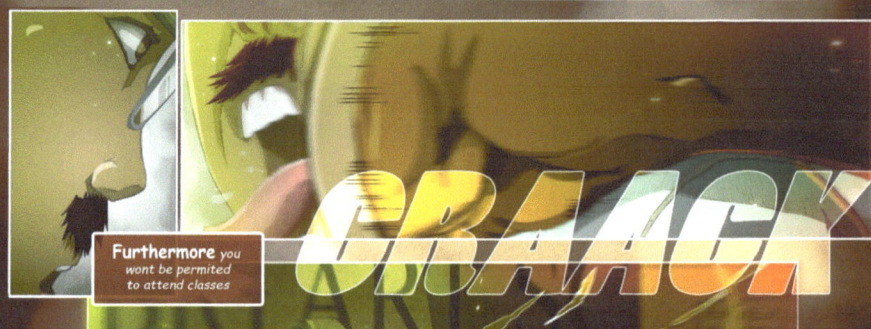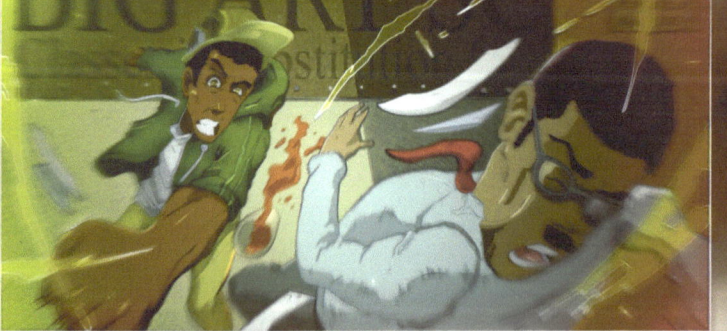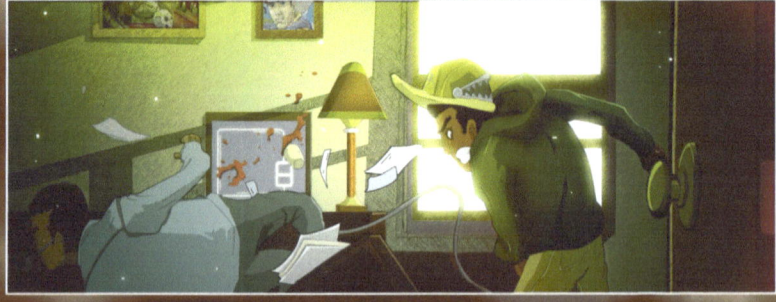

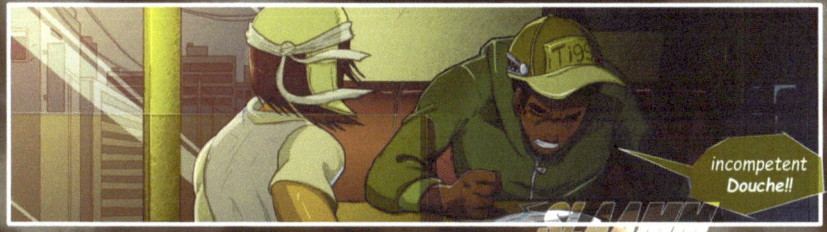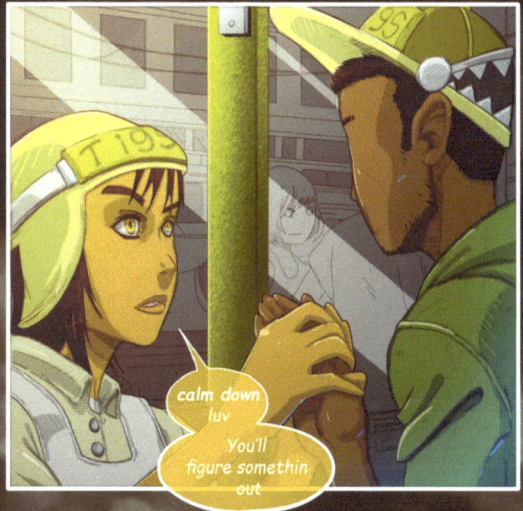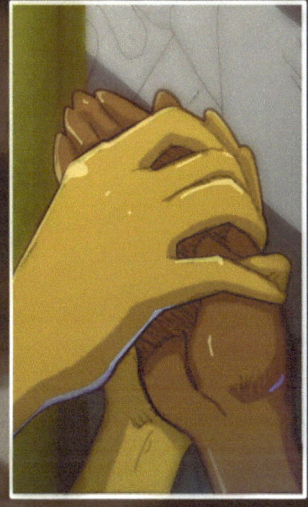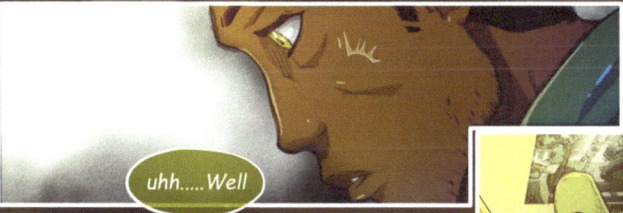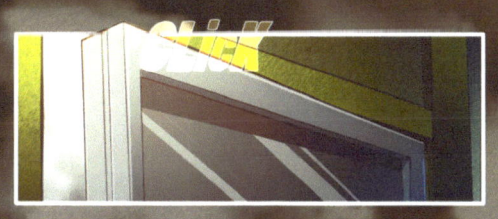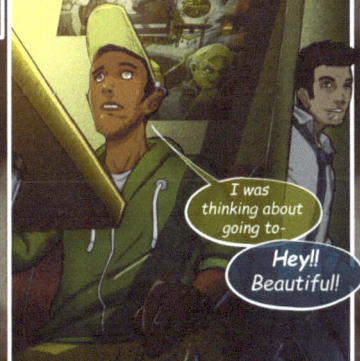

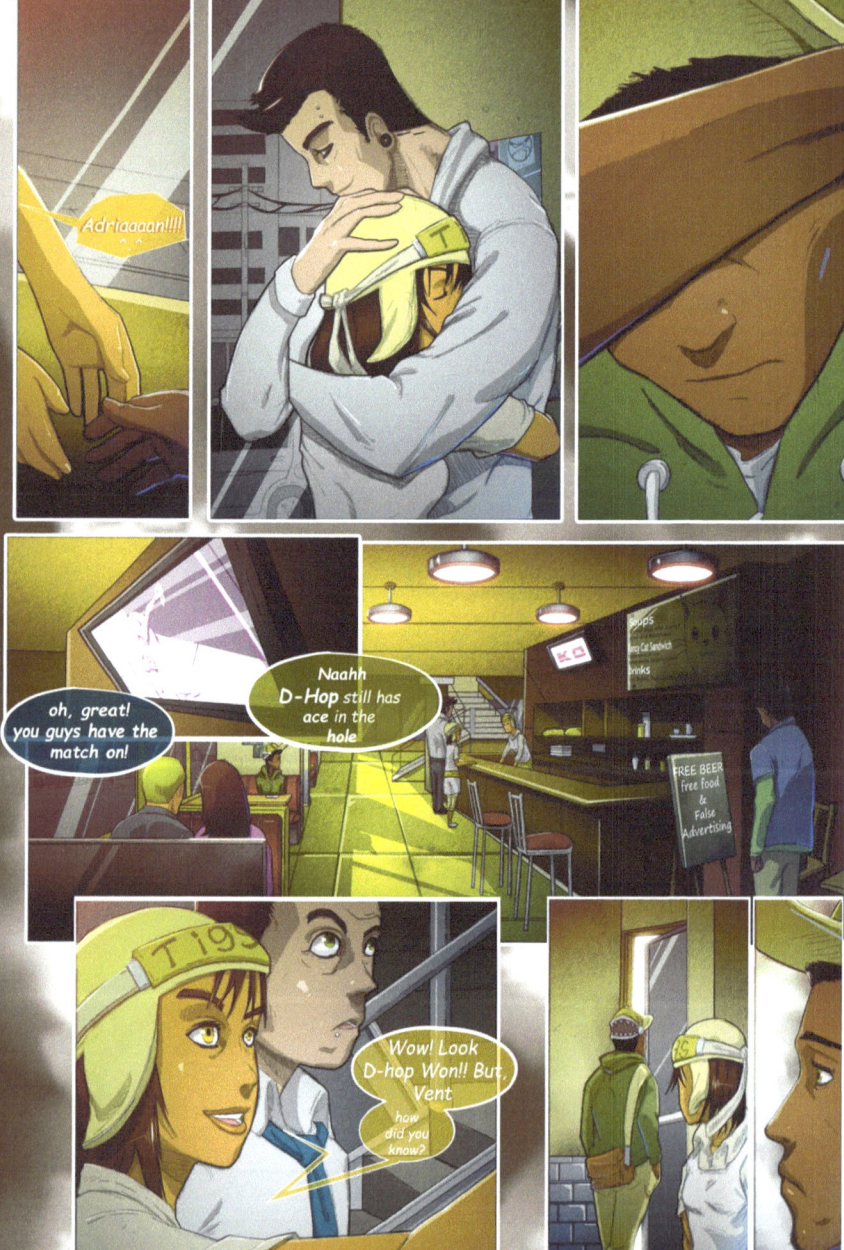

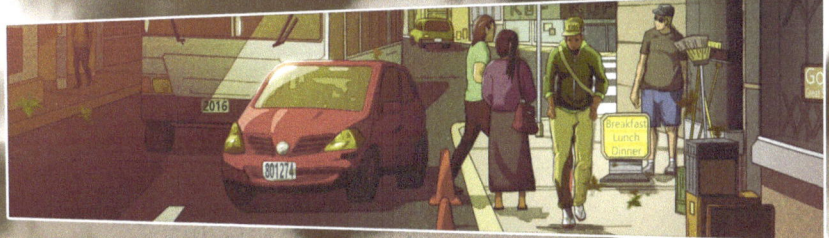
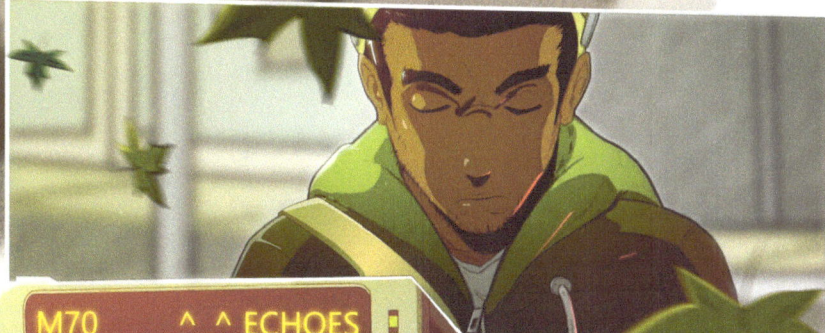
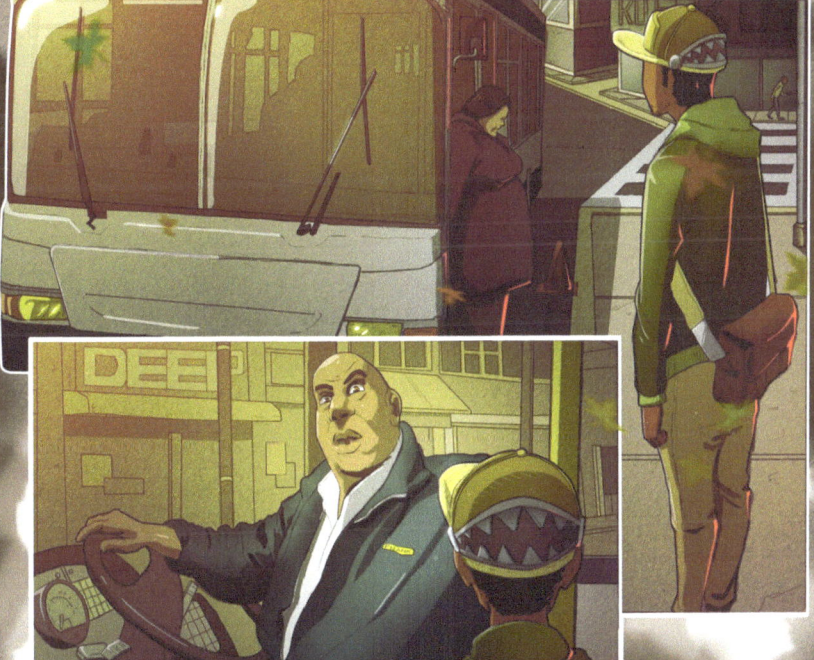

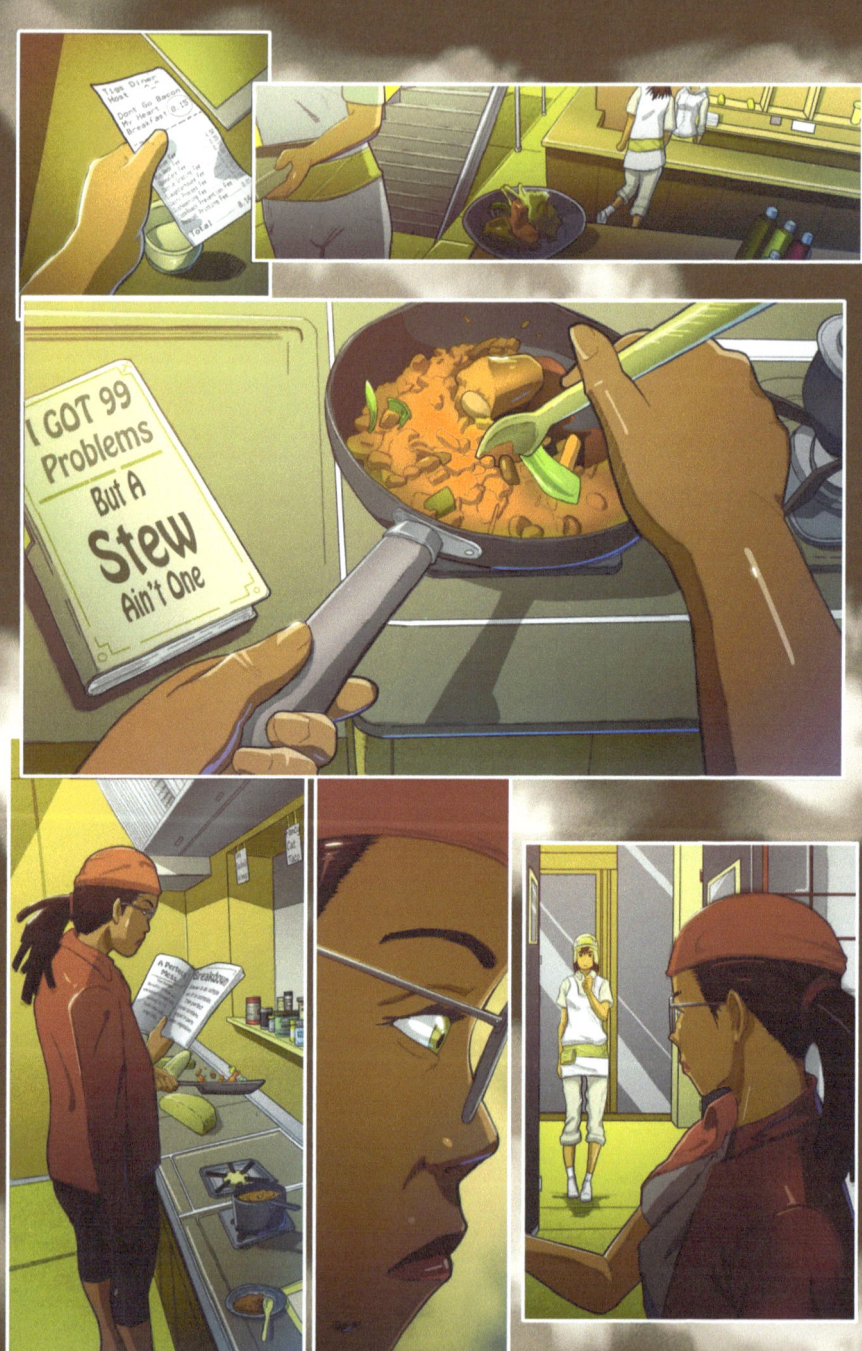

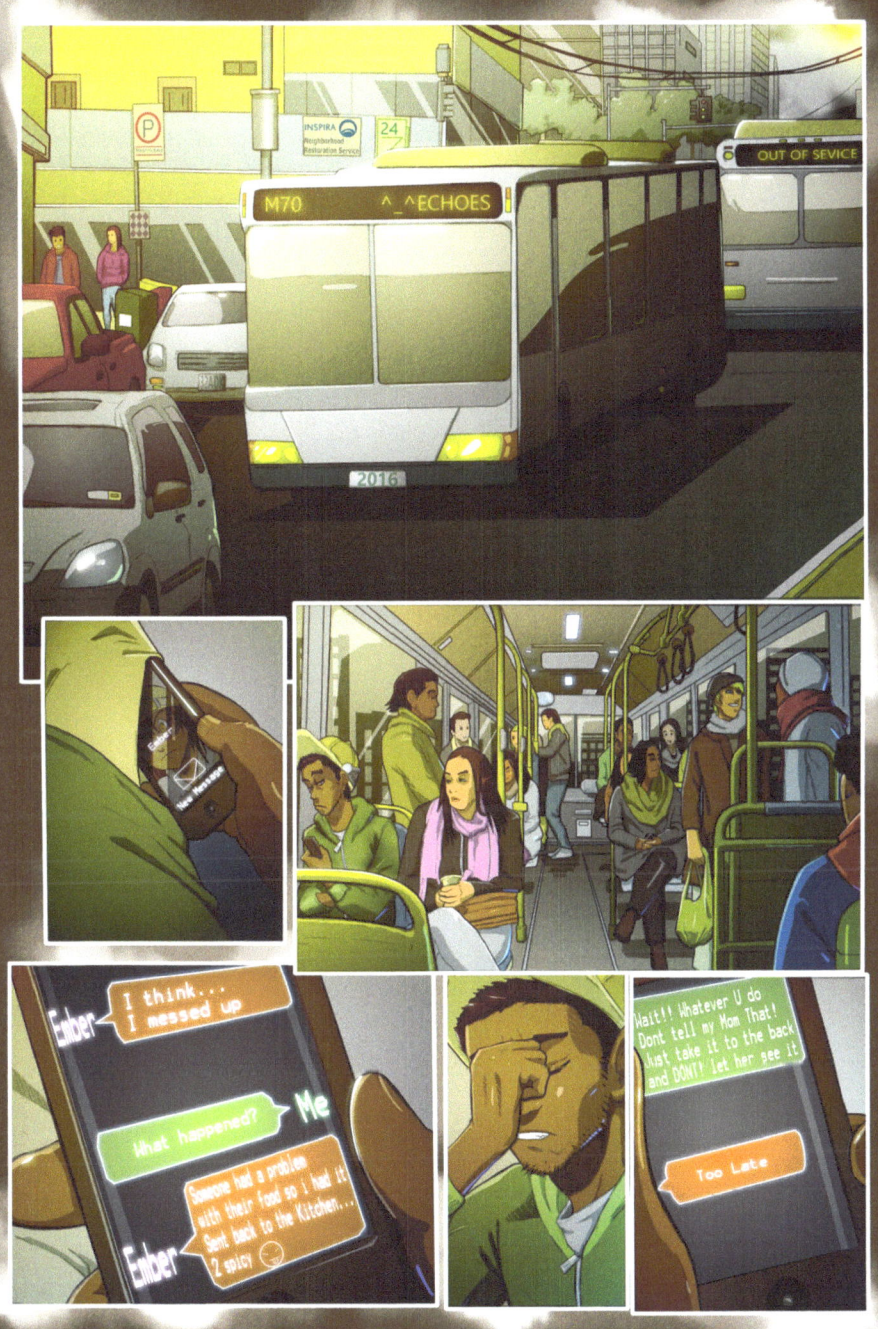

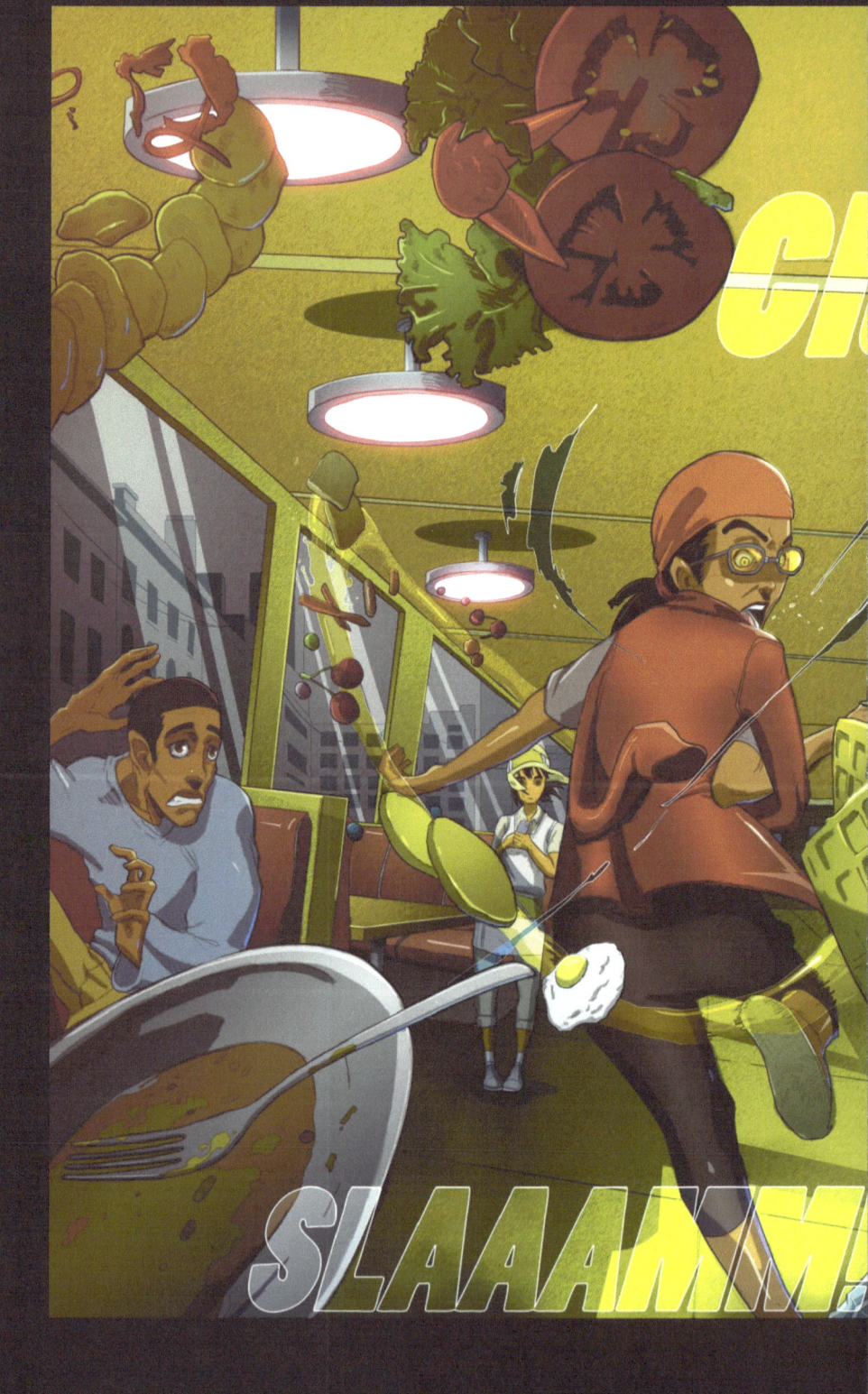

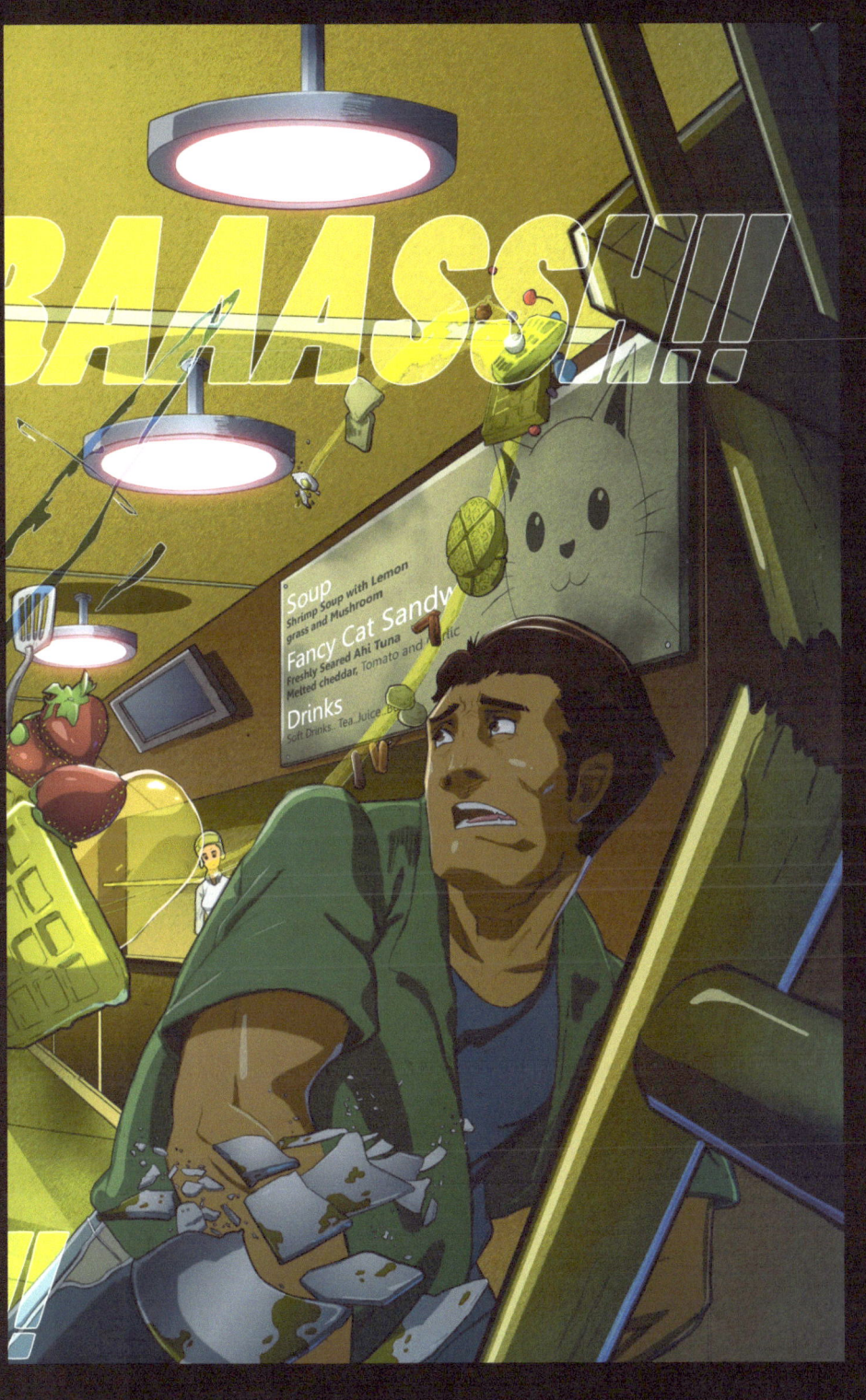

CHRIS GOODING Gallery showcase

NAME - Christopher Gooding
LOCATION - DALLAS, TEXAS
WEBSITE - TWITTER.COM/CHRISGOODCOMICS, INSTAGRAM.COM/CHRISGOODINGCOMICS
MAJOR PROJECTS - MUDBRUSH, TUNE, NO PARKING, THE SINGULARITY, FRANKENSTIEN SAMURAI

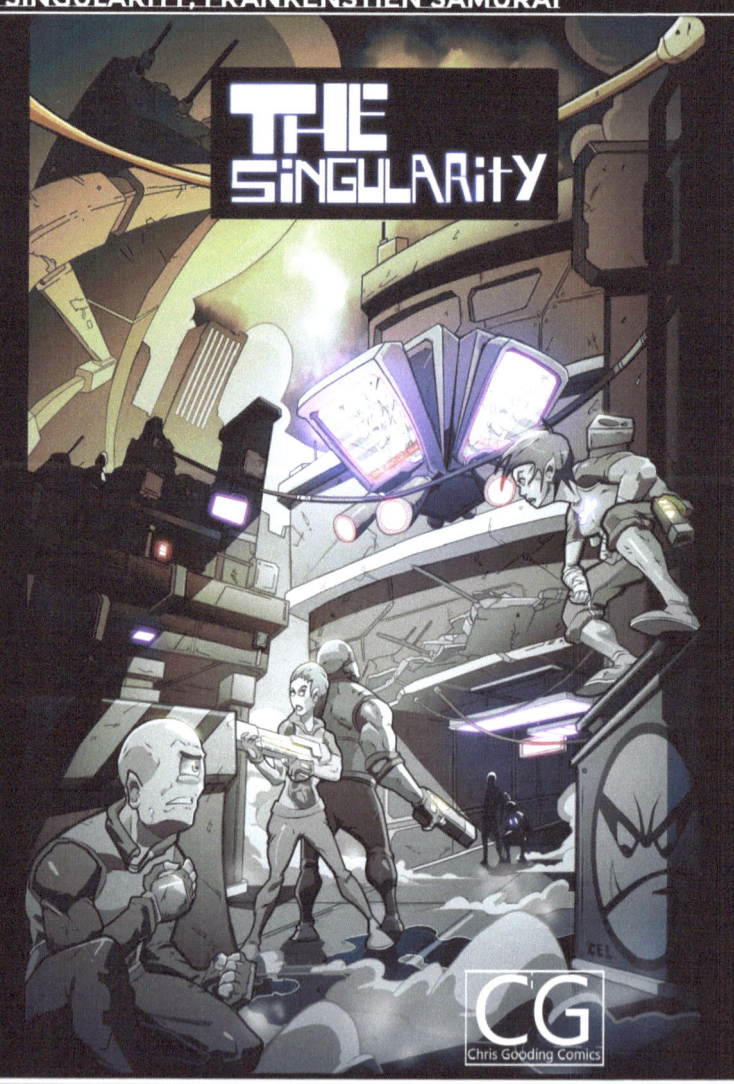

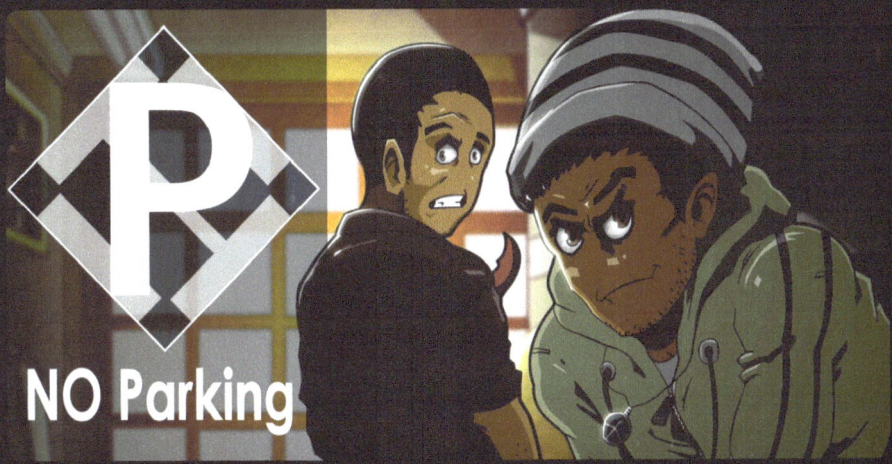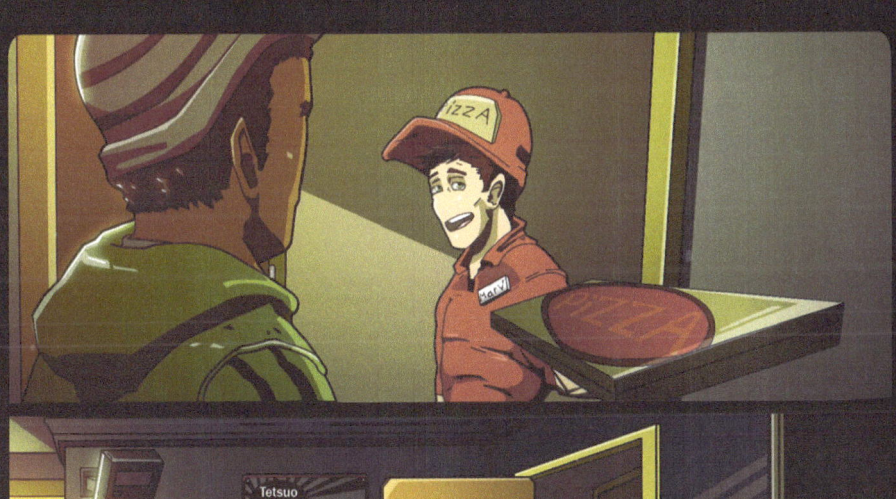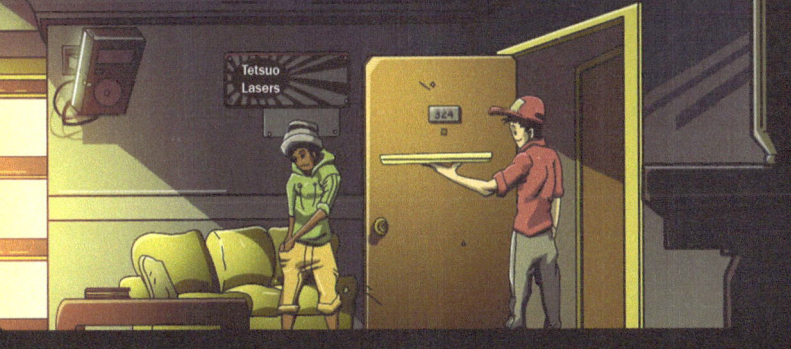

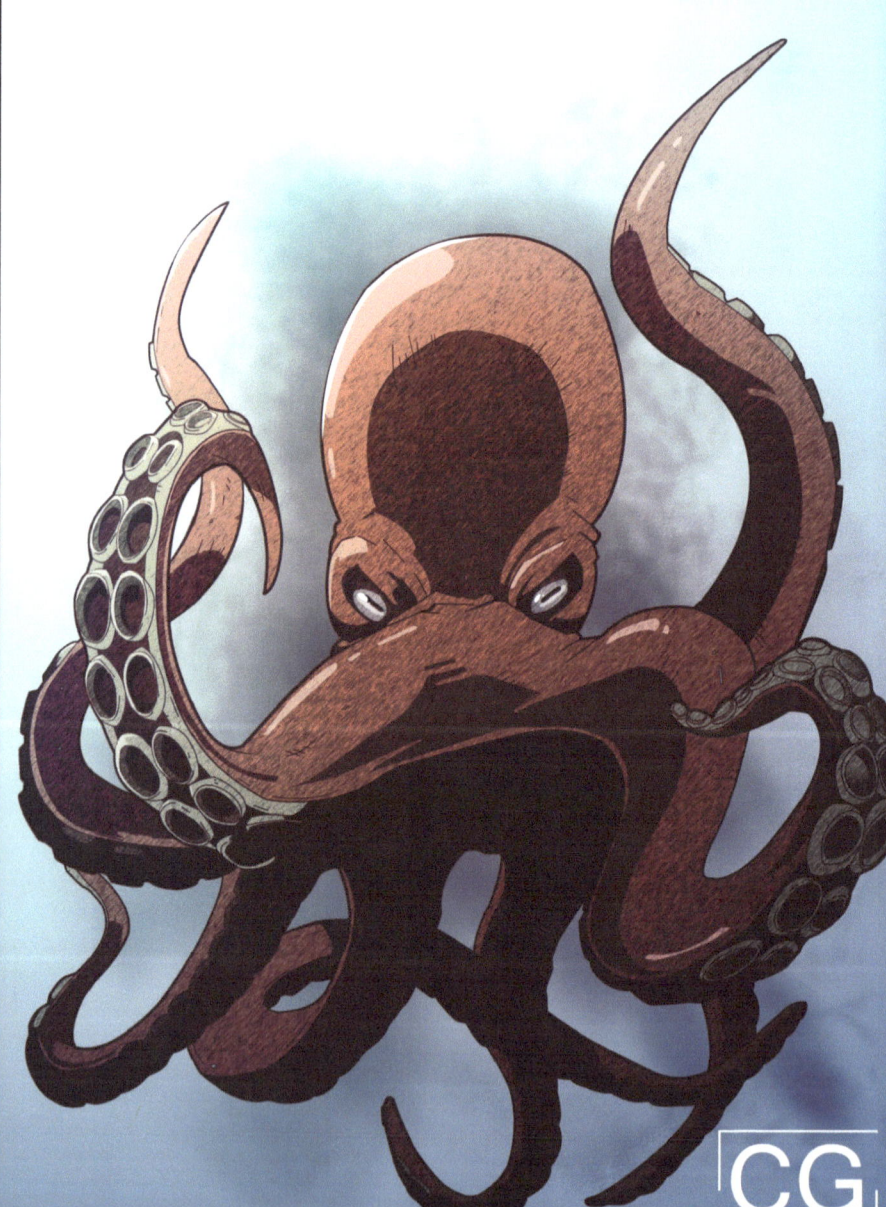

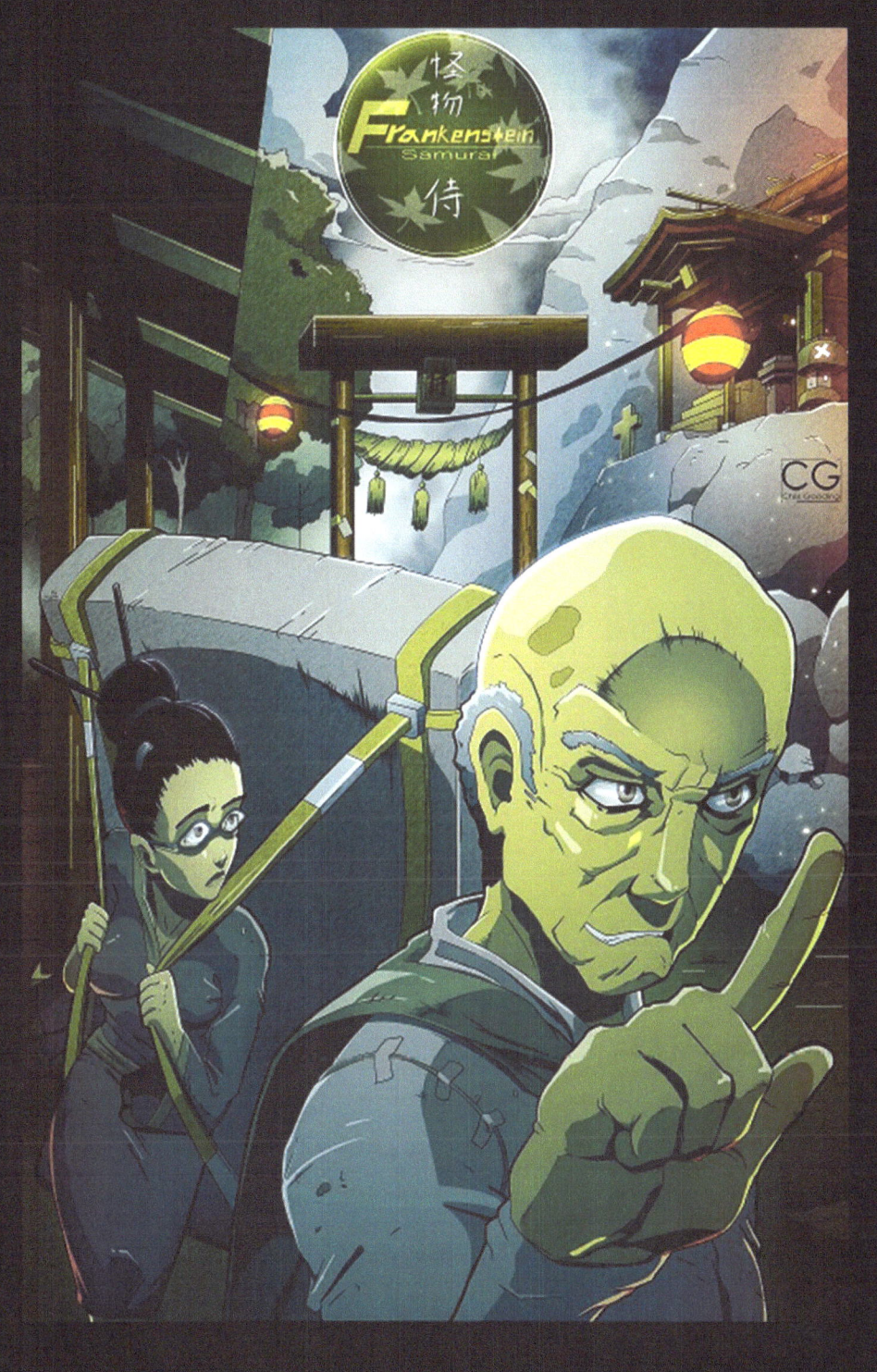

Before and After

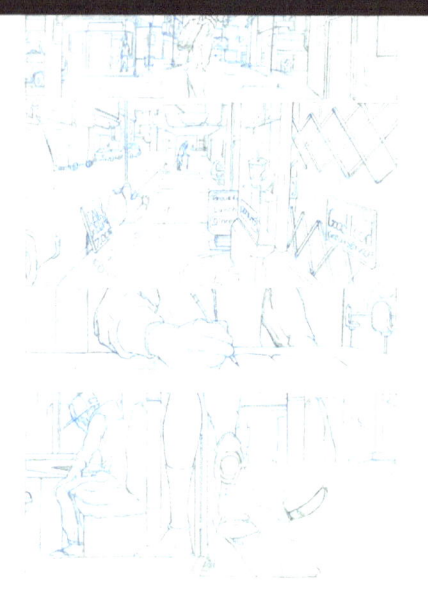
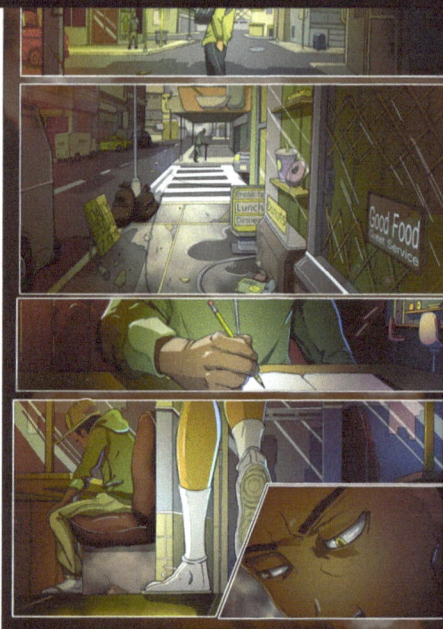
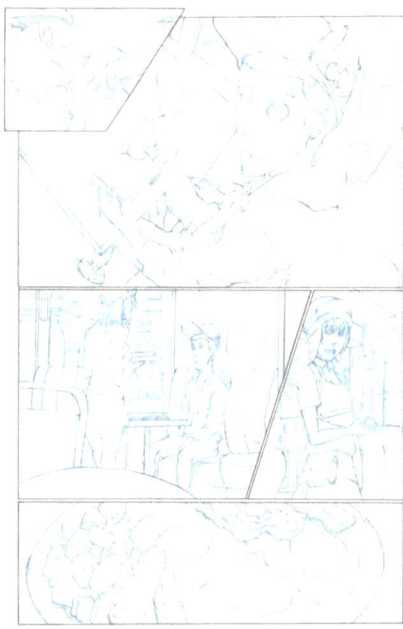
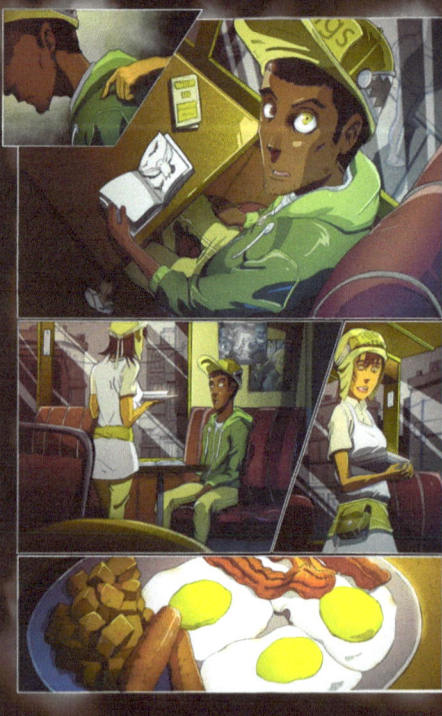

Before and After

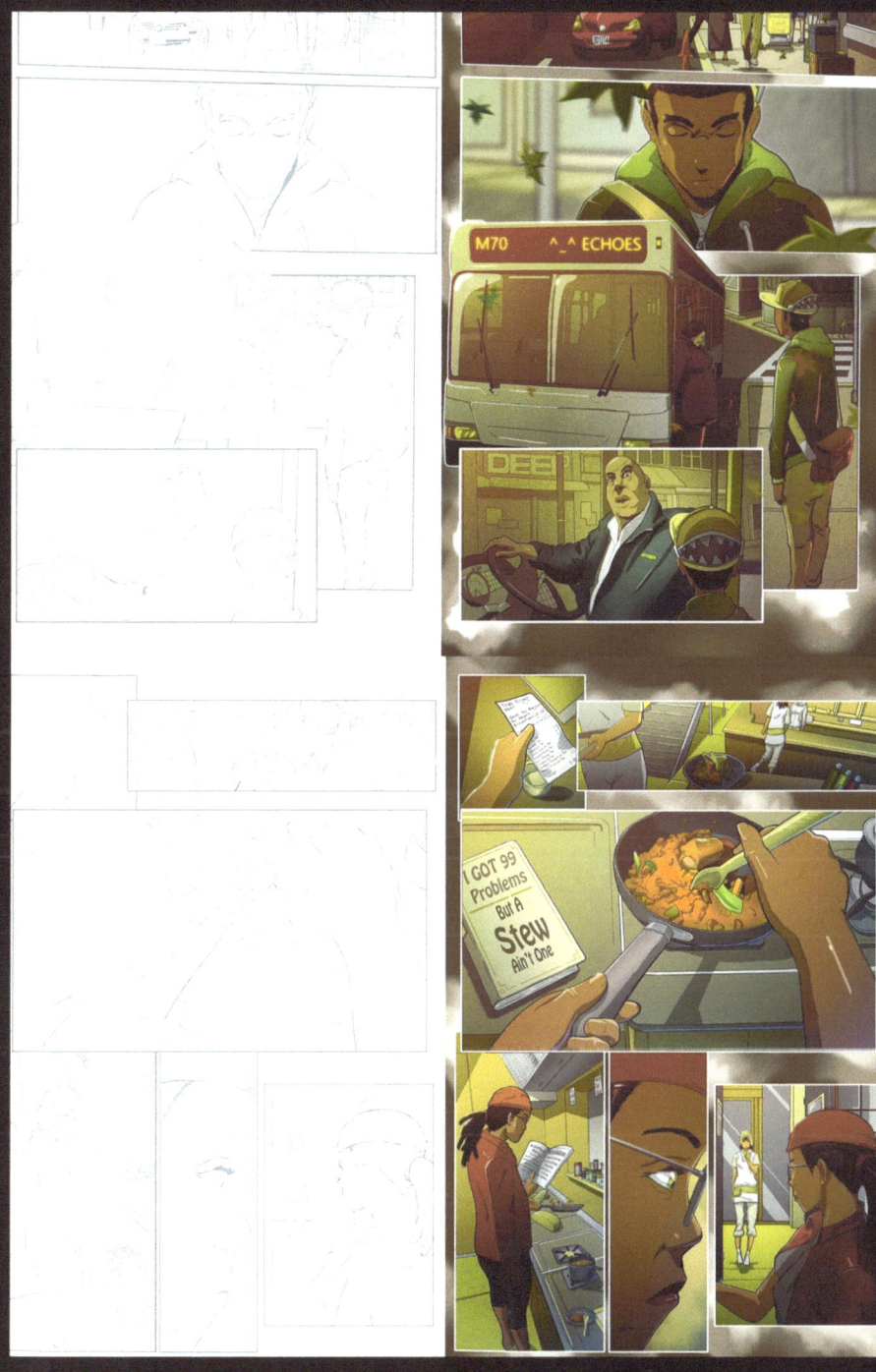

Before and After

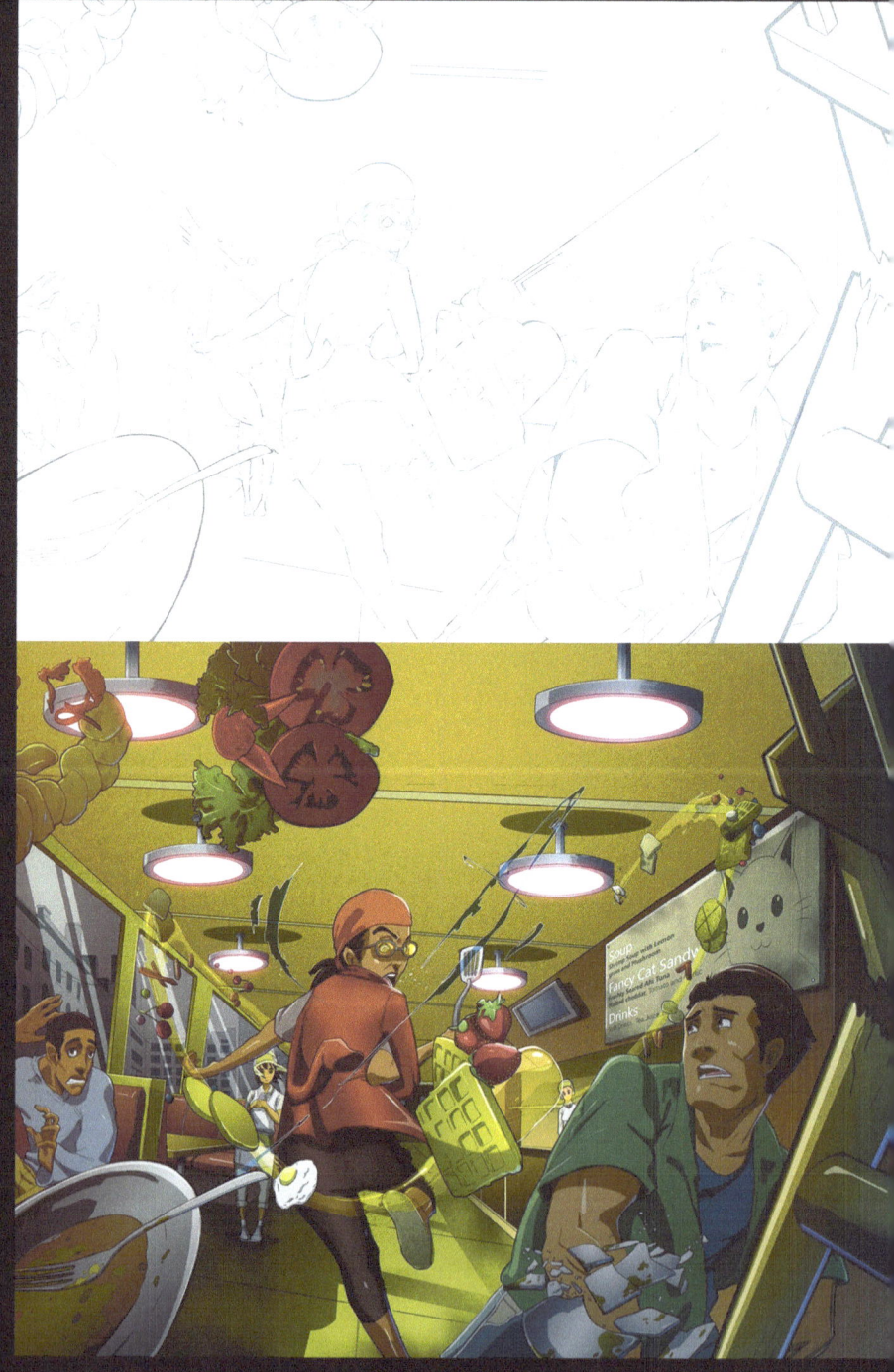

Before and After

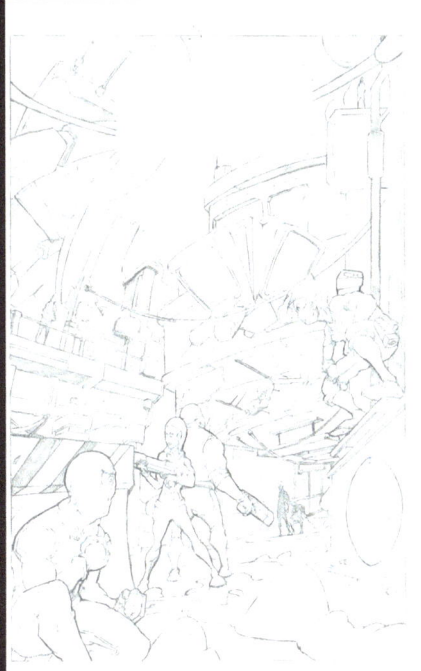
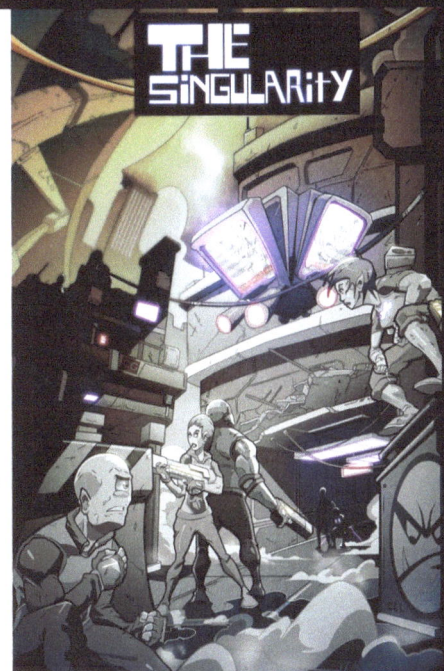
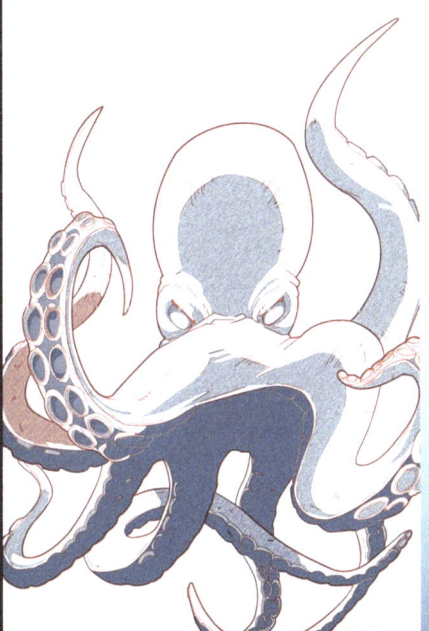
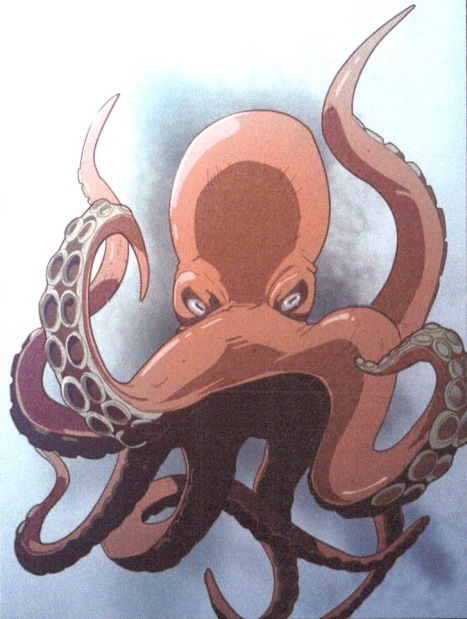

TUTORIAL Chris Gooding on Illustration

STEP 1

Right from the start I knew I wanted to keep things simple.
A one character composition with a good amount of detail
In his clothing and expression.
I start by drawing the character one layer at a time.
I Use whatever free drawing apps are available in the App Store.
They're are a lot of options,
shop around a little and find the one you like the best.
I used a combination of sketch book pro and photoshop to create this

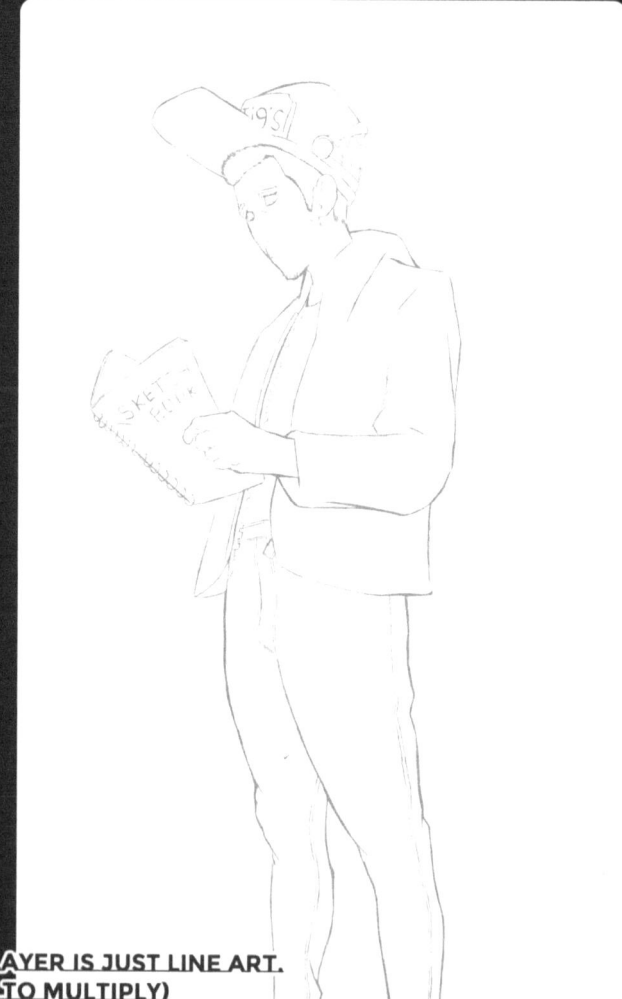

THE FIRST LAYER IS JUST LINE ART.
(SET LAYER TO MULTIPLY)

TUTORIAL
Chris Gooding on Illustration

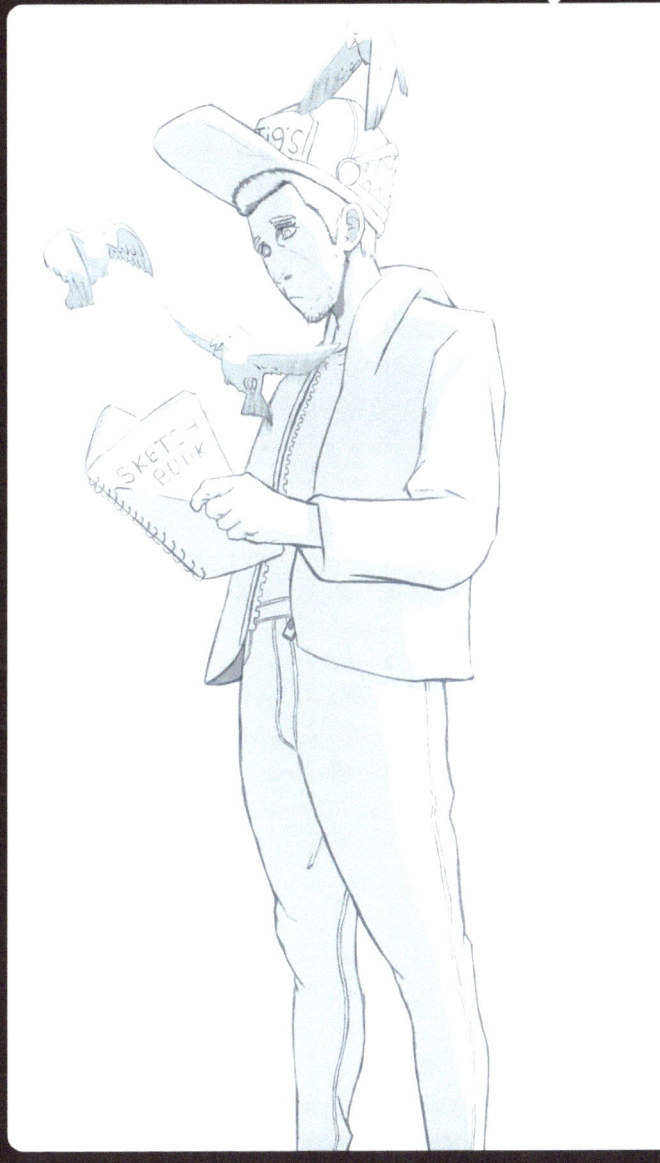

STEP 2
**I ADDED SOME BIRDS
THEN I ADD 2 LAYERS OF SHADOW
(SET LAYERS TO MULTIPLY)**

TUTORIAL   Chris Gooding on Illustration

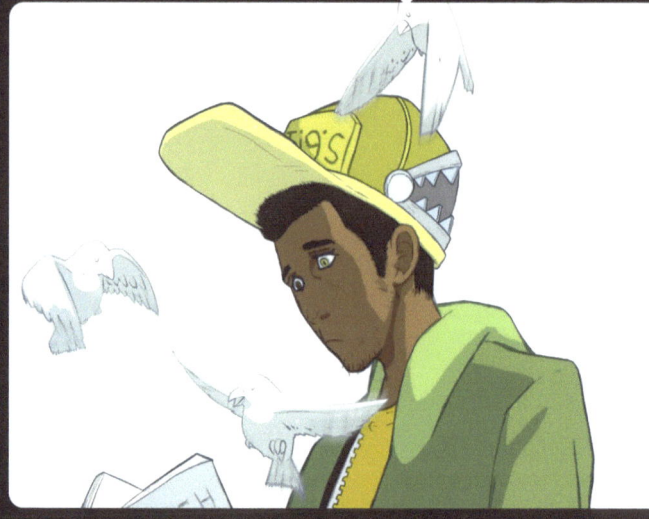

Step 3

After that I export the art
into photoshop.
Photoshop gives you more
options and it lets you control
The resolution of your image

so your art comes out
really sharp and will look
great when
It goes to print

If you don't have access to
photoshop you can use Gimp
(free software).
Or you can just continue in your
drawing app as best you can.

Once i have my image in photoshop
 I set the resolution at 300 dpi

I clean up my line art a little and
I add a layer of flat colour

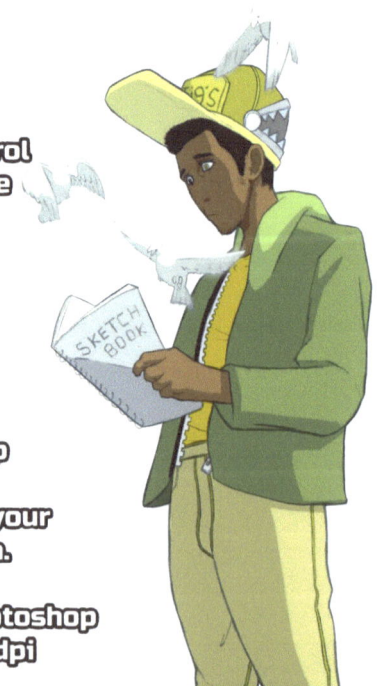

TUTORIAL   Chris Gooding on Illustration

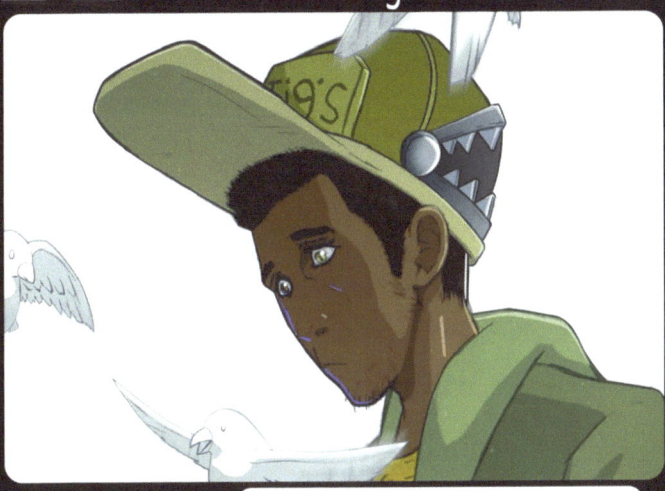

Step 4

Then we add four layers of light.
A combination of soft light,
color dodge, normal, and divide.

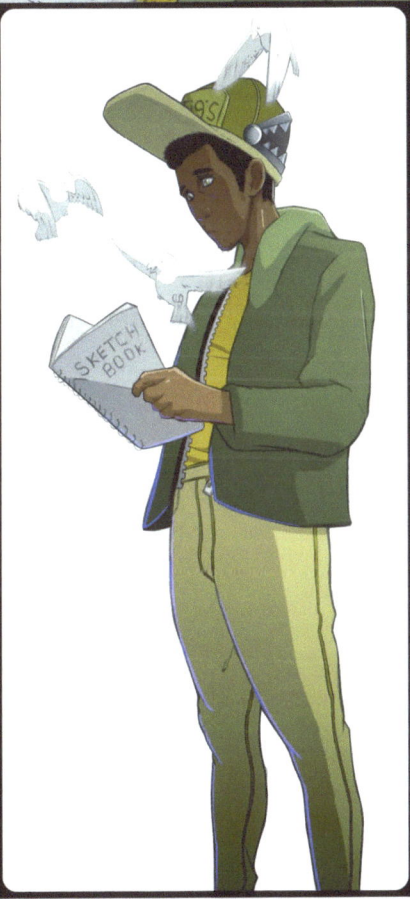

You don't have to add this many
layers of light to complete you art.
You can use 2 layers of soft light
and manipulate the overall
lighting using filters and
lens flares.
Just experiment a little
and find out what works for
you.

TUTORIAL
Chris Gooding on Illustration

Step 5

Now I add my background.

This background is just a collage of panels from my comic book

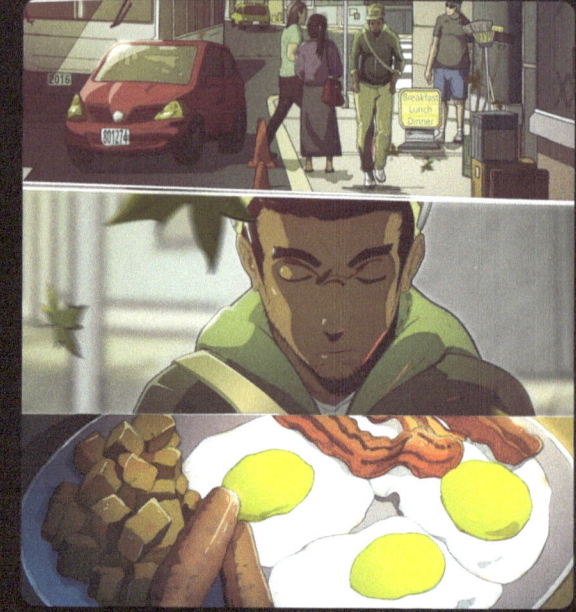

Step 6

I darkened the background layer with another layer I put on top of it for contrast. This layer was filled with a dark grayish blue

(set layer to multiply)
(set opacity to about 57%)

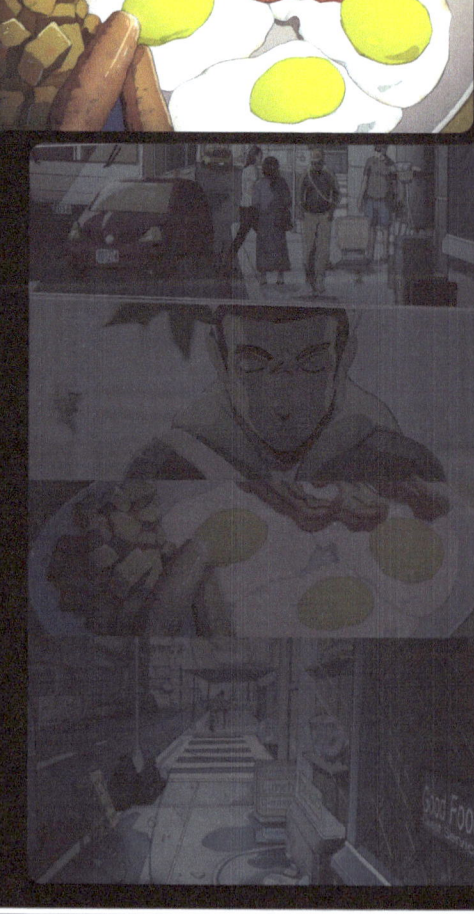

TUTORIAL
Step 7

Chris Gooding on Illustration

I put the whole thing together and dropped in a makeshift logo out of a few layers of text. I also added a thin white outline around the character. That's it
Cover complete and ready for print

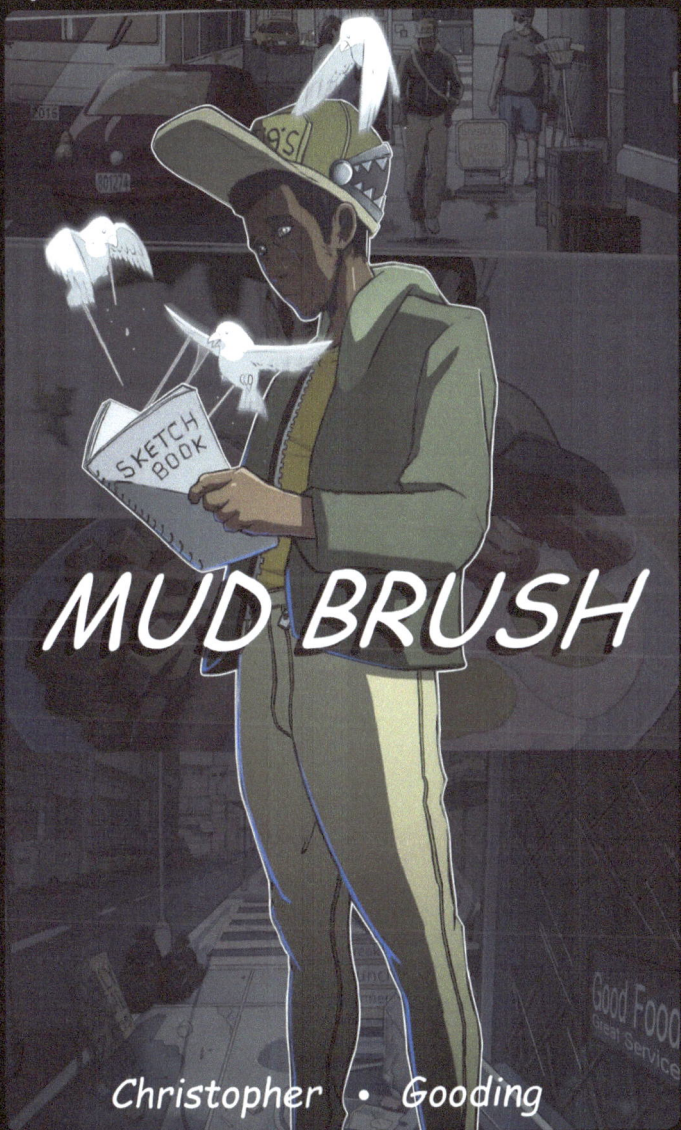

www.ingramcontent.com/pod-product-compliance
Lightning Source LLC
Chambersburg PA
CBHW040349220526
45473CB00009B/2823